Heroes for Young Readers
Activity Guide
for Books 13–16
Jim Elliot • Jonathan Goforth
Cameron Townsend • Lottie Moon

Renee Taft Meloche

YWAM Publishing is the publishing ministry of Youth With A Mission. Youth With A Mission (YWAM) is an international missionary organization of Christians from many denominations dedicated to presenting Jesus Christ to this generation. To this end, YWAM has focused its efforts in three main areas: (1) training and equipping believers for their part in fulfilling the Great Commission (Matthew 28:19), (2) personal evangelism, and (3) mercy ministry (medical and relief work).

For a free catalog of books and materials, contact:

YWAM Publishing
P.O. Box 55787, Seattle, WA 98155
(425) 771-1153 or (800) 922-2143
www.ywampublishing.com

Heroes for Young Readers Activity Guide for Books 13–16
Copyright © 2006 by Renee Taft Meloche

10 09 08 07 06   10 9 8 7 6 5 4 3 2 1

Published by YWAM Publishing
P.O. Box 55787
Seattle, WA 98155

ISBN 1-57658-370-8 (10-digit)
ISBN 978-1-57658-370-8 (13-digit)

Scripture quotations are taken from the Holy Bible, New International Version®, Copyright© 1973, 1978, 1984 by the International Bible Society. Used by permission of Zondervan Publishing House.

All rights reserved. No part of this book may be reproduced in any form without permission from the publisher. Permission is granted to the individual purchaser to reproduce student materials in this book for noncommercial individual or classroom use only. Permission is not granted for schoolwide reproduction of such materials.

Printed in the United States of America.

Contents

Introduction 5

Jim Elliot 7

Jonathan Goforth 23

Cameron Townsend 43

Lottie Moon 59

Can You Name the Hero? 75

Answers to "Can You Name the Hero?" 76

Answers to Questions 77

"I Will Follow" Song 79

Syllabus 80

Introduction

This activity guide is designed to accompany the following books from the Heroes for Young Readers series by Renee Taft Meloche and Bryan Pollard: *Jim Elliot: A Light for God; Jonathan Goforth: Never Give Up; Cameron Townsend: Planting God's Word;* and *Lottie Moon: A Generous Offering.* It provides the Christian schoolteacher, Sunday-school teacher, and homeschooling parent with ways to teach and reinforce the important lessons of these books.

Each book contains the following parts:

- **Coloring Page.** There is a picture of each hero with memorable people and events surrounding him or her for the children to color.
- **Hero Song.** The hero song is a tool to reinforce the main lesson of the hero. Music is often more memorable than spoken or written text.
- **Character Quality.** Each hero is given a character quality for the children to focus on. Discussion questions and visual aids are provided.
- **Character Activity.** The character activity uses drama or arts and crafts to convey more fully the character quality of the hero.
- **Character Song.** The character song encourages children to develop the particular character quality in their own lives.
- **Shoebox Activity.** This activity uses arts and crafts to create a keepsake to remember each hero and how they served. The children will put this keepsake into a shoebox (or other container) so that they will have a treasure box of memories of the heroes.
- **Cultural Page.** This page illustrates something that is representative of the country each hero worked in as a missionary, such as an animal, game, craft, or recipe.
- **Map.** The map page, which the children will color, shows the country or countries the hero lived in growing up and as a missionary.
- **Flag.** A flag (usually of the country the hero worked in as a missionary) is provided for the children to color.
- **Fact Quiz.** This page tests the children's comprehension of each hero story by giving true and false statements inside a particular object that relates to that story. The children will color in the true statements and draw an X over the false statements.
- **Fun with Rhyme.** This page has five stanzas from each hero story. The last word of each stanza is blank, and the children try to fill in the blank, rhyming it with the last word in the second line. A Word Bank is provided for very young readers. (When making copies, the Word Bank can be covered up for the more advanced reader and speller.)
- **Crossword Puzzle.** This page tests the children's comprehension of each story. A Word Bank is provided for young readers. (Again, when making copies, the Word Bank can be covered up.)

- ❖ **Can You Name the Hero?** This exercise has four stanzas, each providing clues about a hero. The children guess which hero each stanza is about.

Before you begin this activity guide, you may want to highlight which activities best suit your needs. For instance, a Sunday-school teacher might want to focus on the coloring pages, songs, character activities, and shoebox activities, while a schoolteacher might want to focus more on the crossword puzzle, fact, map, and cultural pages. A thirteen-week syllabus is included at the end of this activity guide for those parents and teachers who would like a guide to covering some or all of the activities.

Reinforcing stories with fun and creative illustrations, songs, drama, and arts and crafts brings the heroes to life and helps the children remember the important lessons learned through the lives of heroes—ordinary men and women who did extraordinary things with God.

Jim Elliot: A Light for God

Jim Elliot Song

Jim prayed that someday he might go where Christians had not been, for he remembered Jesus' words: be lights before all men.

Jim did not hide his light in school, and everyone who looked could see his Bible on the very top of all his books.

In Ecuador, in Ecuador, Jim was a light in Ecuador. Despite a flood he had no doubt God's flame would not burn out.

In Ecuador, in Ecuador, Jim was a light in Ecuador. He gave up his own very life; for God he sacrificed.

The Good Character Quality of Jim Elliot

Definition of Devotion: Commitment to a purpose no matter how hard things get.

Bible Verse: "Now devote your heart and soul to seeking the LORD your God" (1 Chronicles 22:19).

Materials

- Copy of the crown, strip, and diamond jewel labeled "devotion" on page 12 for each child (use heavy white paper or card stock; if you do not wish to have the children color their crowns, use heavy yellow paper or yellow card stock)
- Scissors
- Crayons or colored pencils
- Stapler
- Double-stick tape or glue

Steps to Follow

1. Introduce the character quality of devotion, which describes Jim, and discuss its meaning with the children. Read aloud the Bible verse above.

2. Have the children color and cut out the diamond labeled "devotion." (Because it is a diamond, tell them they may want to leave the middle part white.)

3. Have the children color and cut out the crown and strip. Read aloud the following Bible verse: "Now there is in store for me the crown of righteousness, which the Lord, the righteous Judge, will award to me on that day" (2 Timothy 4:8).

4. Have the children tape or glue the diamond to the crown. Then have them staple the strip to the crown and put it around their heads. This will serve as their "thinking cap" about devotion.

5. Ask the children, "How did Jim show devotion in his life through his words or actions?"
    - Jim was willing to leave his country and give up the comfortable life he had to live in the jungle.

- ❖ Jim had to learn a new language, get used to new food (even chonta worms), and adjust to a completely new way of living.
- ❖ After Jim lost his hut, clinic, and part of the school and airstrip he had helped build (a whole year's worth of hard work), he started all over again.
- ❖ Jim risked his life for the Auca Indians so that they could know God.

6. Ask the children if they know someone—a parent, neighbor, or friend—who demonstrates devotion. Have them tell the class about this person.

7. Ask the children to think of examples in their own lives when they have shown devotion or how they would like to be more devoted, such as:
   - ❖ Politely eating the dinner that is served you at someone else's house
   - ❖ Regularly attending church
   - ❖ Cleaning up after a sick pet

8. Have the children sing the character song "We Will Be Devoted" on page 13. (This song is sung to the tune of "Do Your Ears Hang Low?" If you have the CD for Jim Elliot, you can have the children follow or sing along with this song. At the end of the CD, there is a solo piano accompaniment that the children can sing along with as well.)

Note: This activity carries over into all the hero stories that follow. For each hero, there will be a new character quality inside a different jewel. You can have the children keep adding jewels to the crowns that they've already made or have them make new crowns each time this activity is repeated. Please be aware that the jewels are a fun way to reinforce the lesson, not a suggestion that the children should expect to be rewarded for doing the right thing as Christians.

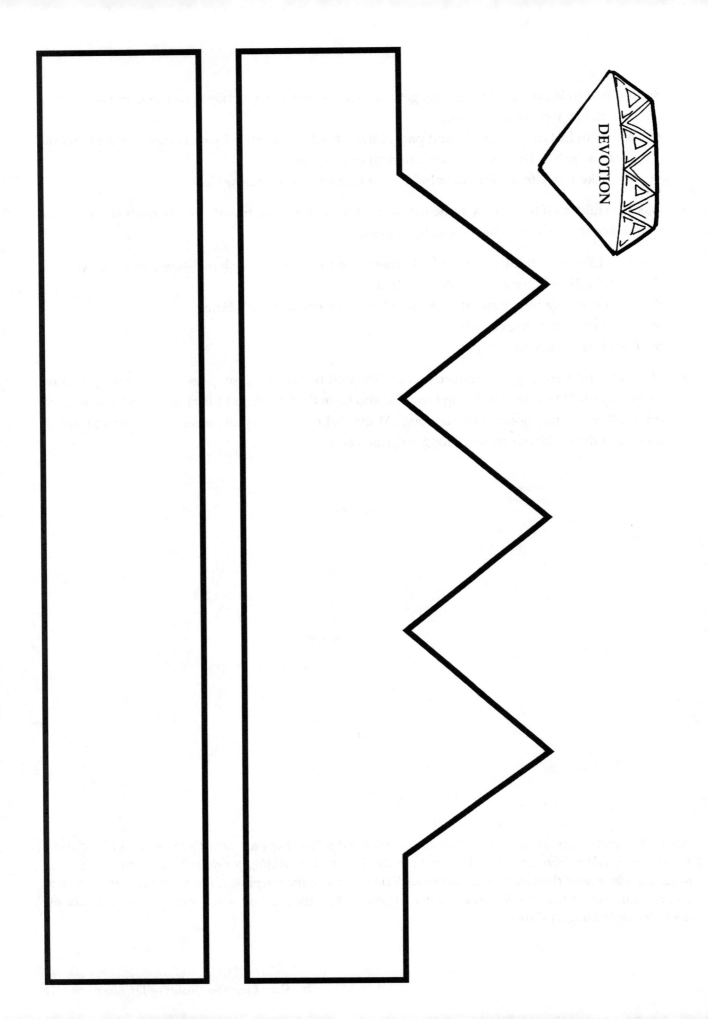

Jim Elliot Character Song
We Will Be Devoted

Character Activity for Jim Elliot
Broadcasting the News

Materials

- Paper
- Pens or pencils
- Large cardboard box with one open side and a square cut in the opposite side to resemble a TV screen
- Two long, thin sticks to represent a TV antenna
- Aluminum foil
- Colored pencils, crayons, or magic markers
- Sheet or blanket

Steps to Follow

1. Have the children review the ways Jim Elliot showed devotion in his life, such as:
   - Jim was willing to leave his country and give up the comfortable life he had to live in the jungle.
   - Jim had to learn a new language, get used to new food (even chonta worms), and adjust to a completely new way of living.
   - After Jim lost his hut, clinic, and part of the school and airstrip he had helped build (a whole year's worth of hard work), he started all over again.
   - Jim risked his life for the Auca Indians so that they could know God.

2. Tell the children they are going to make a television set out of a box. Have them make it look like a TV by drawing features (on the side with the "screen" cut out of it) such as a power button and volume and channel controls.

3. Wrap two sticks with aluminum foil and push them into the top of the TV box to serve as antennas.

4. Set the TV on a table that has been draped with a sheet or blanket.

5. Have the children put their head inside the box just behind the square opening and "broadcast" about the life and death of Jim Elliot and the ways he showed the Indians how devoted he was to them.

Shoebox Activity for Jim Elliot
Eating with the Indians and Making an Indian Figure

Part I: Eating with the Indians

Although Jim lost his life to Auca spears, the first Indian tribe he met in Ecuador was gentle, warm, friendly, and helpful (especially during the flood). Like Jim and these Indians, the children can share a friendly jungle meal.

Materials

- A plastic cup filled with papaya juice for each child
- Gummy worms (three or four for each child)
- Oreo cookies (two for each child)
- Plastic knife (one for each child)
- Chocolate pudding cups (one for each child)

Steps to Follow

1. Have the children take their Oreo cookies, remove the white frosting with a plastic knife, crush up the cookies, and put the pieces on top of the chocolate pudding.

2. Have them stick several gummy worms (representing chonta worms) halfway into their chocolate pudding with crushed cookies (representing mud).

3. Now have two of the children pretend to be Jim and Pete and the rest of the children pretend to be Indians. Have the Indians warmly greet Jim and Pete and invite them to eat their snack of papaya juice and chonta worms with them.

Caution: Some children, because of health reasons, should not be given certain foods. Please take all necessary precautions, including asking each child's parent or guardian for permission to give the child these foods.

Part II: Making an Indian Figure

Materials

- Toilet paper tube (one for each child)
- 5.5 x 4 inch piece of brown paper (one for each child)
- Construction paper

- ❖ Feathers
- ❖ Chenille stems (also called pipe cleaners)
- ❖ Scissors
- ❖ Party picks (long toothpicks)
- ❖ Crayons, colored pencils, or markers
- ❖ Double-stick tape
- ❖ Glue
- ❖ Pen

Steps to Follow

1. Have the children tape the 5.5 x 4 inch brown paper rectangle around a toilet paper tube, which will represent an Indian figure.

2. Have the children create a face and hair with crayons, colored pencils, or markers.

3. Have the children add decorative items such as feathers and chenille stems.

4. Poke a hole in each child's toilet paper tube (where an Indian might hold a spear) by using the tip of a pen. Then have the children stick a party pick into the toilet paper tube to represent a spear.

5. Have the children put their Indian figures in their shoeboxes, a reminder of how devoted Jim Elliot was to the Indians living in Ecuador.

16 ❖ Shoebox Activity for Jim Elliot

Making Migajon Figures

Migajon is a clay made from bread. Today it is used in Ecuador and throughout Central and South America to make tiny animals, toys, and decorations.

Materials

- Two slices of white bread for each child
- White glue (enough for two tablespoons for each child)
- Paintbrushes
- Acrylic paints
- Newspaper
- Paper towels
- Nearby water faucet
- Optional: Glossy acrylic spray finish

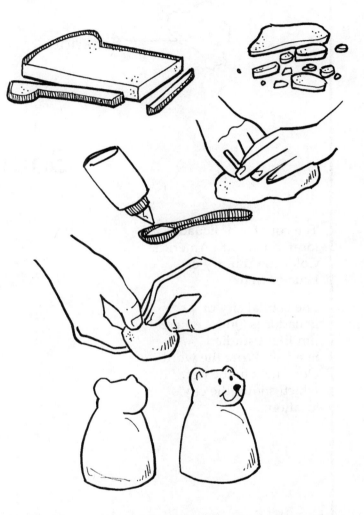

Steps to Follow

1. Cover a table surface with newspaper.

2. Have the children take two slices of white bread each, remove the crust, and tear the bread into small pieces.

3. Have the children mix two tablespoons of white glue into the bread with their hands. It will be very sticky at first, but after a few minutes of kneading the stickiness will disappear and the mixture will become smooth and clay-like.

4. Have the children wash their hands and dry them with paper towels. Then have them shape the clay into small dishes or tiny animals.

5. *Optional:* If time permits, let the clay sculptures air dry, or bake them in an oven at 250 degrees. If you bake them, check them regularly since the size and thickness will determine how long each piece should be heated. If you do not have time, proceed to the next step.

6. Have the children paint the dishes and animals with acrylic paints.

7. *Optional:* Spray each piece with one coat of glossy acrylic finish when dry.

Map: Jim Elliot

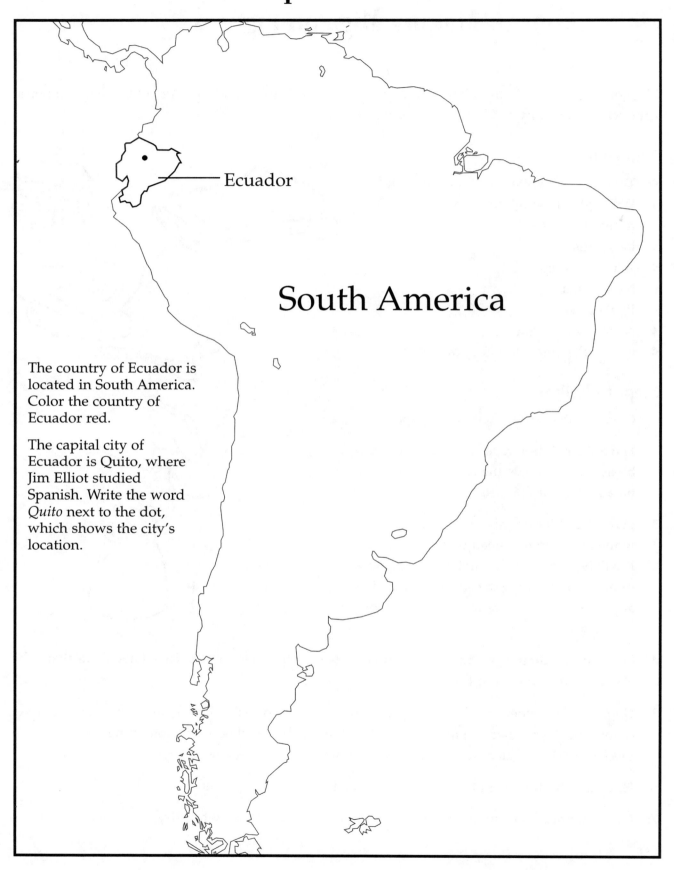

The Flag of Ecuador

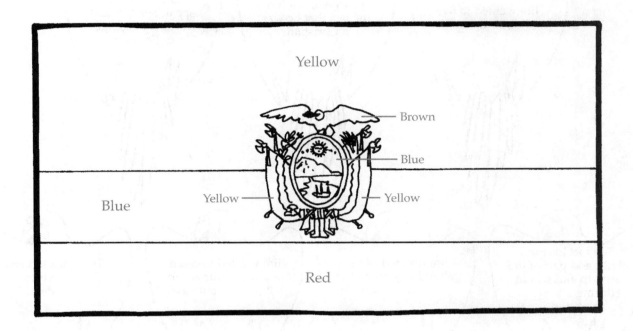

Above is the flag of Ecuador. Color the flag red, blue, yellow, and brown where indicated.

Jim Elliot Quiz

Color the parrots whose facts are correct.
Draw a big X over the parrots whose facts are incorrect.

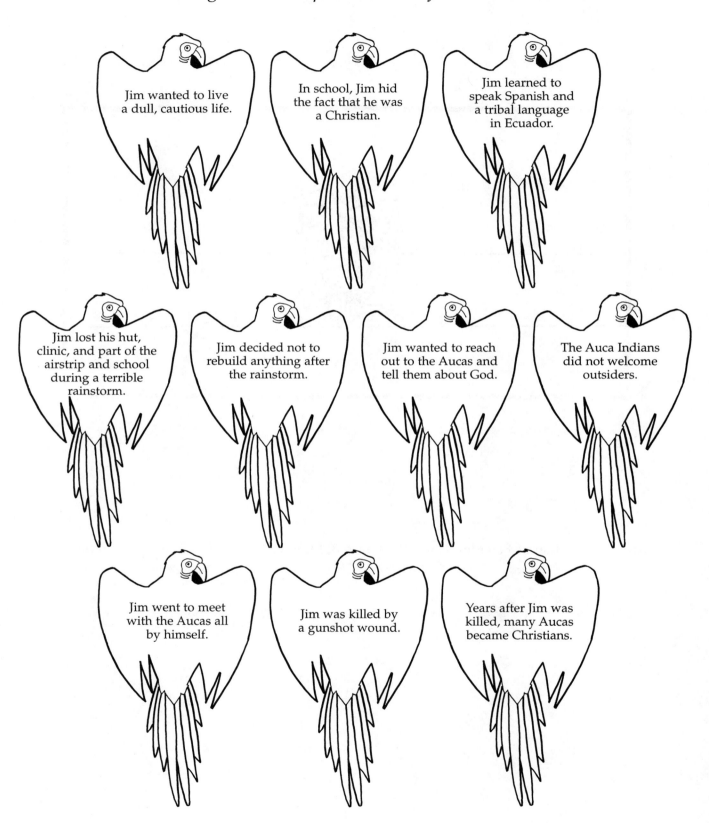

Fun with Rhyme

It's your turn to be a poet. See if you can fill in the correct word inside each parrot by using the word bank and without looking at your book on Jim Elliot. Hint: The word will rhyme with the last word in the second line.

Word Bank

| shine |
| out |
| ground |
| say |
| need |
| few |

When Jim was home, his father, an
  evangelist, would read
him stories of brave people who
  risked much for those in _____.

Jim's father, too, encouraged him
  in missions, since he knew
that Christian workers all around
  the world are very _____.

Huge kapok trees stood high above.
  Bright birds made squawking sounds.
As monkeys swung from tree to tree,
  snakes slithered on the _____.

A whole year's work that they had done
  had all been washed away.
The two men stood in silence; there
  was nothing they could _____.

While their bright flame was somewhat dimmed,
  the two men had no doubt—
they would not quit, they would rebuild.
  Their light would not burn _____.

Like Jim we all can make a difference
  in our own lifetime.
If we love God and others too,
  our lights will brightly _____.

Jim Elliot Crossword Puzzle

Word Bank

shine
chonta
Aucas
Quito
Oregon
helicopter
spear
Ecuador
kapok
baptized

Across

3. A type of tree found in the jungle.
6. The country in South America where Jim worked as a missionary.
7. Aucas became Christians and were _ _ _ _ _ _ _ _.
8. Like Jim, our lights should brightly _ _ _ _ _.
9. The city in Ecuador where Jim studied Spanish.
10. The weapon that killed Jim.

Down

1. The name of the Indians who were feared.
2. A kind of worm found in the jungle.
4. A rescue team searched for Jim by planes and by _ _ _ _ _ _ _ _ _ _.
5. The state in America where Jim was from.

Jonathan Goforth: Never Give Up

Jonathan Goforth Song

In Bible school, young Jonathan had classmates who were mean, and yet he was determined not to give up on his dream.

And so he stayed and studied hard until his school was done so he could go to China and could teach about God's Son.

In China, in China, he went to preach in China. When students heard the things he knew, respect for him soon grew.

In China, in China, he went to preach in China. When he went blind and could not see, he still served faithfully.

The Good Character Quality of Jonathan Goforth

Definition of Determination: Doing all you can to achieve your goals despite difficulties.

Bible Verse: "I am determined to be wise" (Ecclesiastes 7:23).

Materials

- Copy of the crown, strip, and emerald jewel labeled "determination" on page 28 for each child (use heavy white paper or card stock; if you do not wish to have the children color their crowns, use heavy yellow paper or yellow card stock)
- Scissors
- Crayons or colored pencils
- Stapler
- Double-stick tape or glue

Steps to Follow

1. Introduce the character quality of determination, which describes Jonathan, and discuss its meaning with the children. Read aloud the Bible verse above.

2. Have the children color and cut out the emerald labeled "determination." (Because it is an emerald, you may want to suggest they color it green.)

3. Have the children color and cut out the crown and strip. Read aloud the following Bible verses: "Do you not know that in a race all the runners run, but only one gets the prize? Run in such a way as to get the prize. Everyone who competes in the games goes into strict training. They do it to get a crown that will not last; but we do it to get a crown that will last forever" (1 Corinthians 9:24–25).

4. Have the children tape or glue the emerald to the crown. Then have them staple the strip to the crown and put it around their heads. This will serve as their "thinking cap" about determination.

5. Ask the children, "How did Jonathan show determination in his life through his words or actions?"

- ❖ When Jonathan's classmates were mean to him in college, he was still determined to finish school and become a missionary.
- ❖ When students mocked Jonathan in China, he refused to give up on them until he won them over.
- ❖ When one young Chinese man was beaten by his father, Jonathan went to his village, determined to change the father's mind.
- ❖ When Jonathan lost his vision, he was determined to keep preaching and teaching.

6. Ask the children if they know someone—a parent, neighbor, or friend—who demonstrates determination in his or her life. Have them tell the class about this person.

7. Ask the children:
   - ❖ Have you ever quit something because you were bullied?
   - ❖ Why do people bully others? Do you think it's to get something they want or, by putting you down, to feel better about themselves?
   - ❖ What do you think you should do if someone is bullying you or someone you know?
   - ❖ Do you think other people's bad attitudes should make us give up when we know we are doing the right thing?

8. Have the children sing the character song "We Will Be Determined" on page 29. (This song is sung to the tune of "Do Your Ears Hang Low?" If you have the CD for Jonathan Goforth, you can have the children follow or sing along with this song. At the end of the CD, there is a solo piano accompaniment that the children can sing along with as well.)

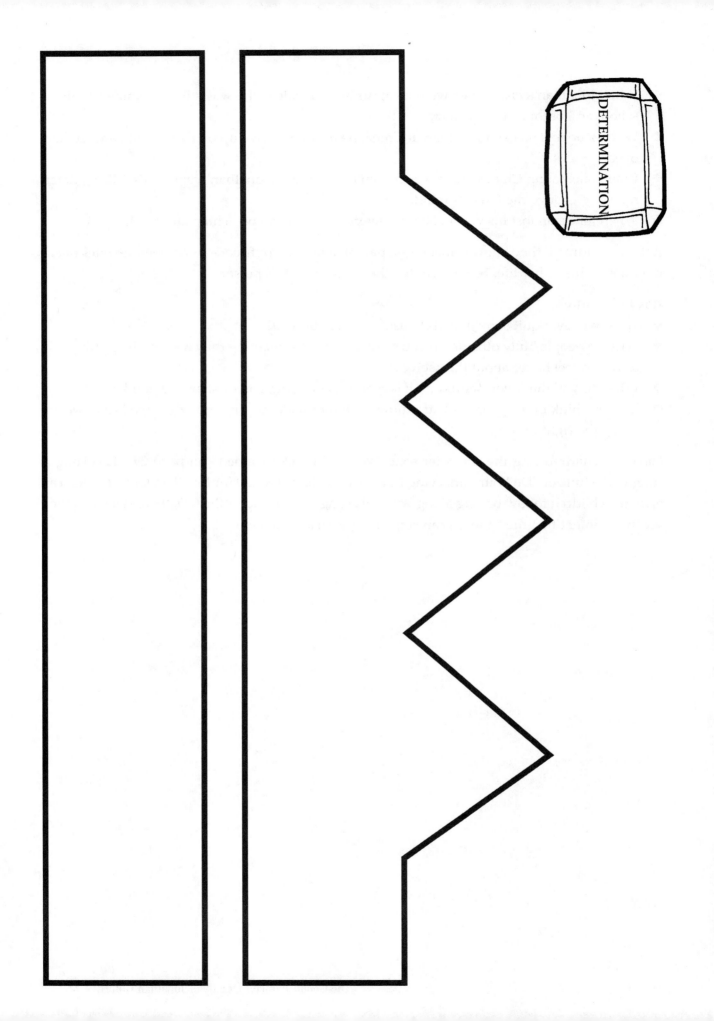

Jonathan Goforth Character Song
We Will Be Determined

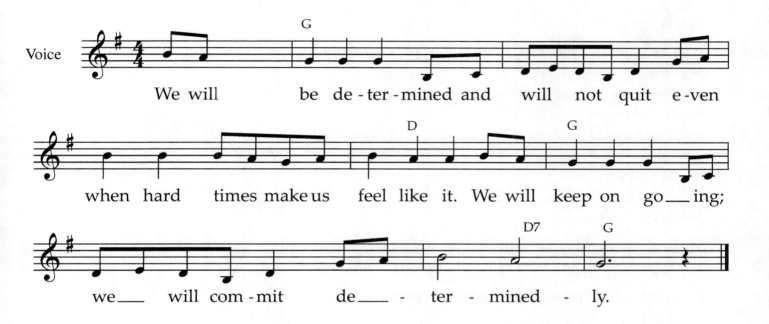

Character Activity for Jonathan Goforth
Practicing Determination

Materials

- 3 oz. paper cup for older children; 8 oz. paper or styrofoam cup for younger children
- Yarn
- 5 x 12 inch piece of aluminum foil (one for each child)
- Masking tape
- Straightened paper clip
- Ruler
- Scissors

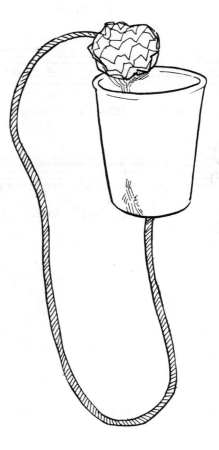

Steps to Follow

1. Puncture a hole in the bottom of the cup with a straightened paper clip. (An adult should do this for very young children.)

2. Cut about 14 inches of yarn and tie a knot at one end.

3. Thread the yarn through the bottom of the cup from the inside so the knot is in the cup.

4. Tape the knot in place for added strength (this can be done on the inside or outside of the bottom of the cup).

5. Shape the foil into a small ball wrapped tightly around the end of the yarn.

6. Now try to swing the ball into the cup. See who can be the most determined to get the ball into the cup five times in a row or the most times out of ten.

7. Sing the character song "We Will Be Determined" on page 29. (This song is sung to the tune of "Do Your Ears Hang Low?" If you have the CD for Jonathan Goforth, you can have the children follow or sing along with this song. At the end of the CD, there is a solo piano accompaniment that the children can sing along with as well.)

8. *Optional:* Repeat this activity but make the yarn longer to make the game more difficult.

Shoebox Activity for Jonathan Goforth
Making Panda Bears

Pandas are large, shy, cuddly-looking Chinese bears with big heads, heavy bodies, round ears, and short tails. They are white with black patches around the eyes, ears, shoulders, chest, legs, and feet. Their coloring helps to hide them in a snowy, rocky environment. Unlike other bears, the panda has unusual catlike eyes and has very good eyesight. The Chinese people call the panda a "giant bear cat."

Pandas eat bamboo shoots and leaves. They are good tree climbers and sometimes take naps high in the trees. Their thick, woolly fur is waterproof and keeps them warm in the cold and wet mountains in central and western China, where they live. There are about 1,000–1,500 pandas living in the wild today, and they live to be about 35 years old.

Materials

- A copy of the panda bear parts and two rectangles (on the following page) on white construction paper for each child
- Toilet paper tube (one for each child)
- Crayons or colored pencils
- Scissors
- Glue
- Double-stick tape
- Construction paper

Steps to Follow

1. Cut out the panda bear parts.

2. Cut out and then tape or glue the large, white rectangle around the toilet paper tube to cover it. The tube represents the panda's body.

3. Cut out and then tape or glue the smaller, black rectangle around the middle of the tube.

4. Now tape or glue the head to the end of the tube and the arms and legs to the sides.

5. Have the children put their panda bears into their shoeboxes as a reminder of how Jonathan went to China and served the Chinese people.

The Canadian Beaver

Jonathan Goforth grew up in Canada, which is part of North America. There are lots of beavers in Canada, and they are the largest rodents in all of North America. A beaver has almost no neck and has very short legs, which make it walk very slowly on land. The beaver is a strong, graceful swimmer, however, and can move very fast in the water. Its hind feet are very large, with five long webbed toes that work like flippers. The beaver uses its tail like a rudder to steer it in the water. The beaver's small, beady eyes enable it to see well in and out of the water.

When frightened, a beaver will slap the water with its tail, making a loud noise, warning other beavers that danger is near. The noise is so loud it can even scare away other animals that might want to attack. The beaver's teeth are long and sharp and are so strong that a beaver can cut down a tree with them. Beavers are wonderful builders; they make dams for shelter and protection against other animals.

Materials

- Two copies of the circles labeled "head/chin" and "muzzle" (on page 35) on brown construction paper for each child
- One copy of the ears, teeth, eyes, and nose (on page 36) on white construction paper for each child
- Scissors
- Double-stick tape, glue, or glue sticks
- Black, light-brown, and dark-brown crayons or colored pencils

Steps to Follow

1. Color the smaller ear circles light brown.

2. Color the larger ear circles dark brown.

3. Color the smaller eye circles black. Leave the larger eye circles white.

4. Color the nose circle black.

4. Take two copies of the circle labeled "head/chin" and color them brown.

5. Take two copies of the circle labeled "muzzle" and color them black.

6. Cut out the two colored copies of the "head/chin" circle and glue them, slightly overlapping, one on top of the other.

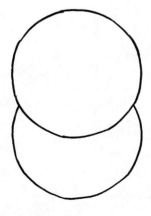

33

7. Cut out all four ear circles and glue the small, light-brown circles onto the larger dark brown circles. Glue them onto the top of the top circle.

8. Cut out the two square teeth and glue them toward the bottom of the bottom circle.

9. Take the two colored copies of the circle labeled "muzzle" and cut them out. Then glue them, slightly overlapping, onto the head and chin circles to make a muzzle.

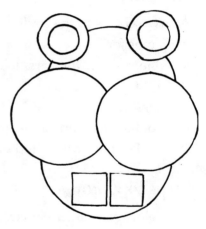

10. Cut out the two eye circles and nose circle and glue them onto the beaver's muzzle.

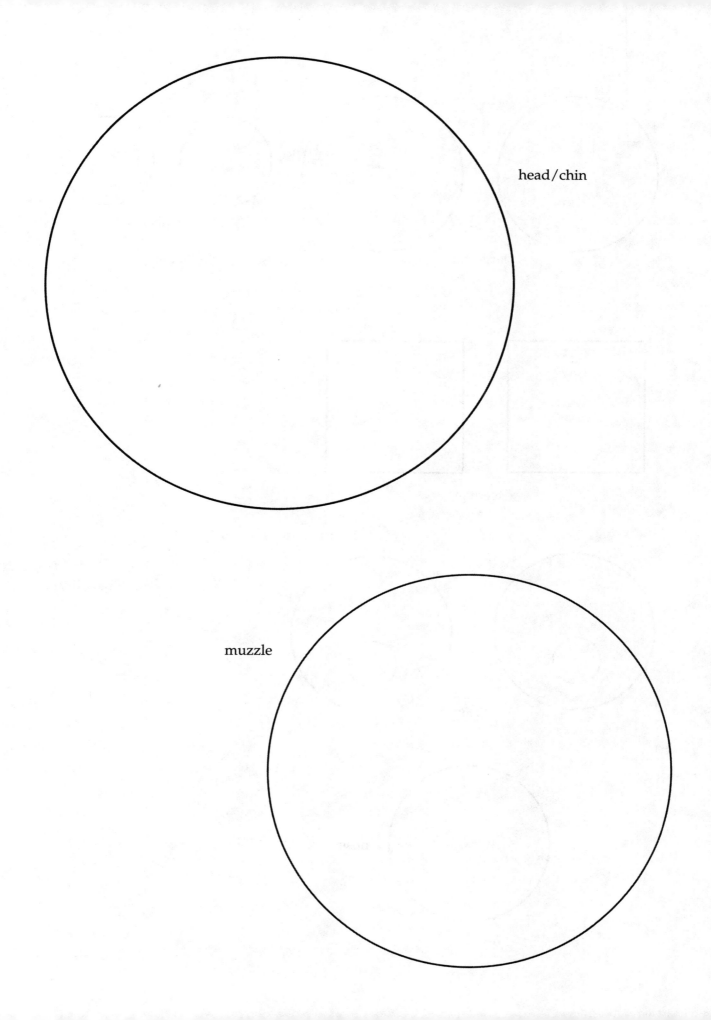

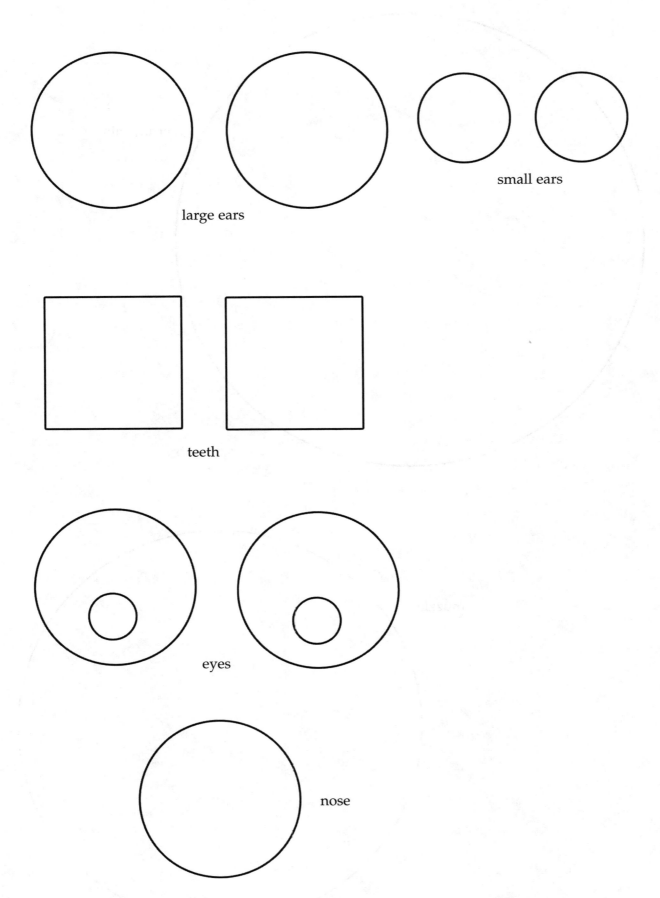

Map: Jonathan Goforth

On the map, find Canada, where Jonathan Goforth grew up, and color it in.

Now find China, where Jonathan lived as a missionary, and color it in.

The Flag of Canada

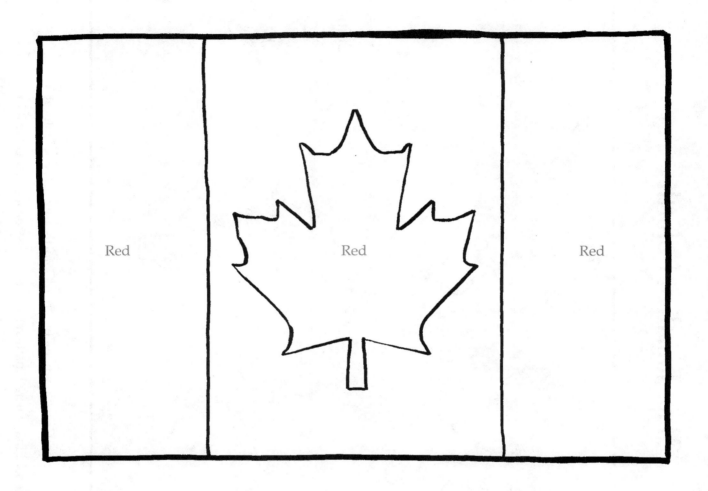

Above is the flag of Canada. Color the flag red where indicated.

Jonathan Goforth Quiz

*Color the pandas whose facts are correct.
Draw a big X over the pandas whose facts are incorrect.*

Fun with Rhyme

It's your turn to be a poet. See if you can fill in the correct word inside each panda bear by using the word bank and without looking at your book on Jonathan Goforth. Hint: The word will rhyme with the last word in the second line.

Word Bank

| good |
| sun |
| met |
| go |
| Son |
| right |

His classmates lined the hall and kicked
   and pushed him to and fro
till they grew tired of their game,
   unbound him, let him _____.

Determined, he would stay and study
   hard till school was done
so he could sail to other lands
   and teach about God's _____.

Upon his graduation, though,
   he could not leave just yet,
for first he married Rosalind,
   an artist whom he'd _____.

They traveled into China and
   they built a home of wood.
The Chinese came to visit, which
   made both of them feel _____.

The students laughed at Jonathan
   though he had just begun;
he told them how the earth can turn
   and move around the _____.

Though Jonathan knew ridicule,
   mockery, and spite,
he did not quit; instead he did
   what God's Word says is _____.

Jonathan Goforth Crossword Puzzle

Word Bank

Chinese
globe
China
Canada
quit
organ
prison
Toronto
Bible
vision

Across

2. The country in North America where Jonathan was from.
3. Something Jonathan refused to do.
4. The name of the city where Jonathan attended Bible school.
6. What Jonathan lost when he was seventy-three years old.
8. A round representation of the earth that Jonathan showed the Chinese students.
9. The country where Jonathan worked as a missionary.

Down

1. A cell-like place with locks and bars that Jonathan visited in Bible school.
2. The language Jonathan learned as a missionary.
5. The kind of stories the Goforths taught the Chinese.
7. An instrument that Jonathan's wife played for the Chinese.

Cameron Townsend: Planting God's Word

Cameron Townsend Song

Young Cameron had always loved to figure out new things like puzzles, riddles, mysteries that could be challenging.

He used his cleverness, and soon he learned how to create new letters for new languages to help him to translate.

It's Wycliffe, it's Wycliffe, the group he formed is Wycliffe, to teach translators other tongues to tell about God's Son.

It's Wycliffe, it's Wycliffe, the group he formed is Wycliffe, so many more could understand in many different lands.

The Good Character Quality of Cameron Townsend

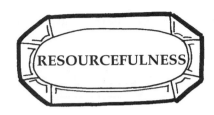

Definition of Resourcefulness: Making the most of what we use.

Bible Verse: "Whoever can be trusted with very little can also be trusted with much" (Luke 16:10).

Materials

- Copy of the crown, strip, and ruby jewel labeled "resourcefulness" on page 48 for each child (use heavy white paper or card stock; if you do not wish to have the children color their crowns, use heavy yellow paper or yellow card stock)
- Scissors
- Crayons or colored pencils
- Stapler
- Double-stick tape or glue

Steps to Follow

1. Introduce the character quality of resourcefulness, which describes Cameron, and discuss its meaning with the children. Read aloud the Bible verse above.

2. Have the children color and cut out the ruby labeled "resourcefulness." (Because it is a ruby, tell them they may want to color it red.)

3. Have the children color and cut out the crown and strip. Read aloud the following Bible verse: "Be faithful … and I will give you the crown of life" (Revelation 2:10).

4. Have the children tape or glue the ruby to the crown. Then have them staple the strip to the crown and put it around their heads. This will serve as their "thinking cap" about being resourceful.

5. Ask the children, "How did Cameron show resourcefulness in his life?"
   - Cameron learned unwritten languages and developed a way to write them down and translate the Bible.
   - Cameron taught the people to read and write by setting up new schools.
   - Cameron formed a group called Wycliffe to train other people to translate also.

- ❖ Cameron used bat dung and pig manure as topsoil to grow fruits and vegetables.
- ❖ Cameron taught the local villagers how to plant and grow food for eating and selling.

6. Ask the children if they know someone—a parent, neighbor, or friend—who demonstrates resourcefulness. Have them tell the class about this person.

7. Ask the children if they can think of ways that they can be resourceful, such as:
   - ❖ Fixing a brother or sister's toy rather than throwing it out
   - ❖ Teaching someone a faster or easier way to do a chore
   - ❖ Experimenting with a science project until it gets results

8. Have the children sing the character song "We Will Be Resourceful" on page 49. (This song is sung to the tune of "Do Your Ears Hang Low?" If you have the CD for Cameron Townsend, you can have the children follow or sing along with this song. At the end of the CD, there is a solo piano accompaniment that the children can sing along with as well.)

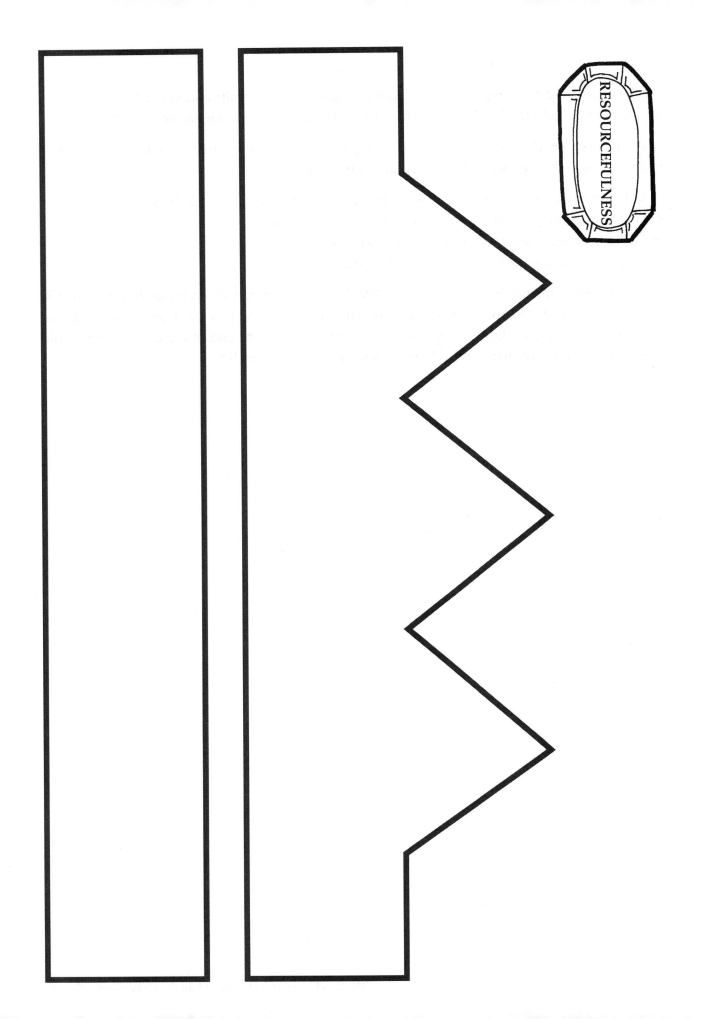

Cameron Townsend Character Song
We Will Be Resourceful

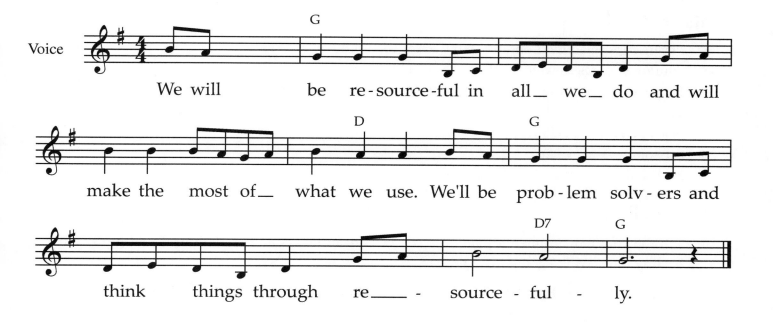

Character Activity for Cameron Townsend
Planting Seeds

Materials
- Plastic cups filled with potting soil (two for each child)
- Sunflower seeds as well as celery, carrot, lettuce, bean, beet, or radish seeds
- Baby carrots, celery stalk, lettuce leaf, beans, beets, or radishes
- One-square-inch Bible (found in Christian bookstores) or a 2 x 3 inch small piece of paper and black pen for each child
- Scissors
- Newspaper (to cover the table surface)

Steps to Follow

1. Tell the children, "Cameron planted seeds of faith in hearts and seeds in soil that grew into healthy foods. We're going to do the same."

2. Have the children choose one kind of seed and plant a few seeds in their plastic cups.

3. On top of the soil in their cups, have the children place a real baby carrot, small stalk of celery, radish, lettuce leaf, bean, or beet, depending on the seed they chose.

4. Have the children take a few sunflower seeds, representing "Seeds of Faith," and plant them into a second cup filled with soil.

5. Give each child a one-inch-square Bible (or have them take a 2 x 3 inch piece of paper, fold it over, and write "Bible" on the front of it) and have them put it in their second cup "garden."

6. Remind the children that while an actual Bible doesn't really grow from seeds, it represents the products that grow from seeds of faith such as love, hope, trust—or good thoughts, good deeds, mature faith—all healthful things.

Shoebox Activity for Cameron Townsend
A Mexican House

Many farmers in Mexico live in small villages. In the dry central part of Mexico the houses are made of adobe, a mixture of mud and clay that is formed into bricks and dried in the sun. The roofs are made from red tiles.

Materials

- Copy of the house and children pattern on the following page for each child
- One 8 oz. milk container for each child
- Penne pasta (long, thin tube pasta)
- Permanent red markers or red tempera paint
- Scissors
- Glue
- Double-stick tape

Steps to Follow

1. Color and cut out the house and boy and girl patterns.

2. Cut the window and the door along the solid lines. (If the children are too young, have an adult do this.)

3. Use double-stick tape to attach the house to a milk carton.

4. Tape or glue the boy and girl patterns to the side or front of the house.

5. With a permanent red marker or red tempera paint, paint enough pasta noodles red to cover the roof.

6. Glue the pasta to the roof to look like red tiles.

7. Have the children put their houses into their shoeboxes as a reminder of how Cameron went to the villages of Mexico to serve the people.

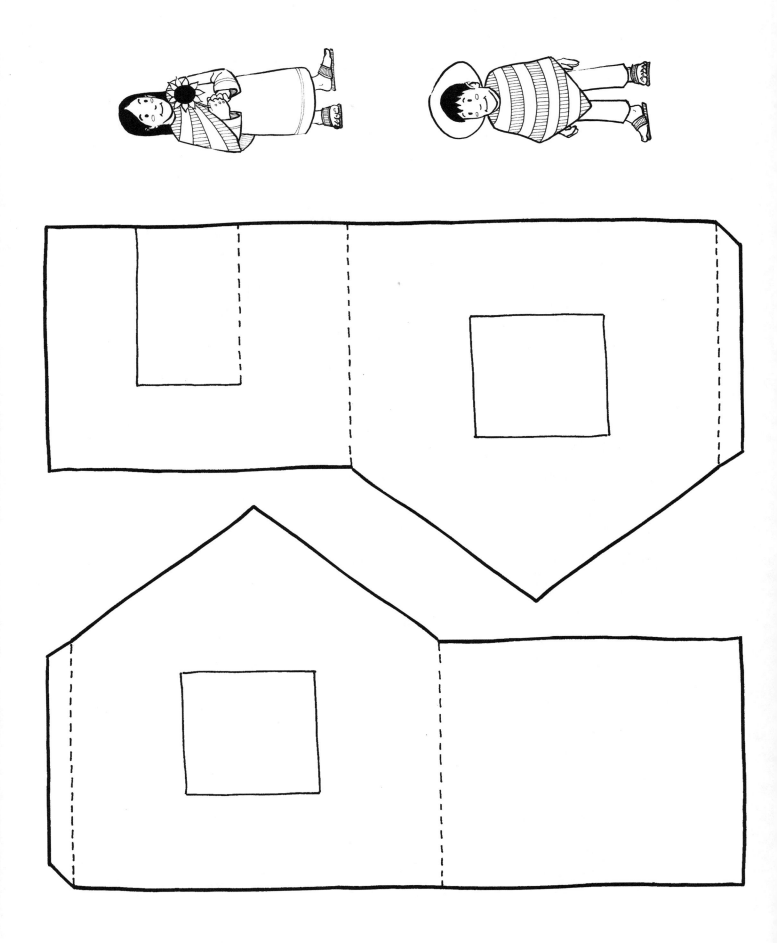

Piñata

Piñatas are brightly colored figures usually made of papier mâché shaped into animals and other things. They are filled with candy, fruit, and toys and are hung from a ceiling or tree. Children, after being blindfolded, take turns trying to hit the piñata with a stick until the piñata breaks and the treats fall out. Throughout Latin America, piñatas are a favorite treat at parties and at special celebrations like Easter and Christmas.

Materials

- Medium-size cardboard box
- Candy
- Tape
- Glue
- Construction paper
- Colored tissue paper
- Crepe paper streamers
- Scarf or handkerchief for blindfold
- Plastic bat
- Rope
- Ziplock bag (one for each child)

Steps to Follow

1. Place candy inside a medium-size cardboard box and tape the opening closed. (Note: Because boxes are thicker than papier mâché, do not tape the box too securely or it will be hard for the children to break open.)

2. Glue construction paper, colored tissue paper, and crepe paper streamers over the entire piñata.

3. Using rope, hang the piñata from a tree or play structure or some secure indoor hanger or hook.

4. Have the children line up in front of the piñata.

5. Tie a blindfold around the eyes of the first child in line and spin him or her around three times. Please note: For very young children you may want to skip this step.

6. While the other children are standing way back, have the child try three times to hit the piñata with a plastic bat.

7. When one of the children hits the piñata hard enough to open it, the candy will pour out for the children to pick up. Have the children put their candy into a ziplock bag to take home.

Caution: Some children, because of health reasons, should not be given certain foods. Please take all necessary precautions, including asking each child's parent or guardian for permission to give the child candy.

Map: Cameron Townsend

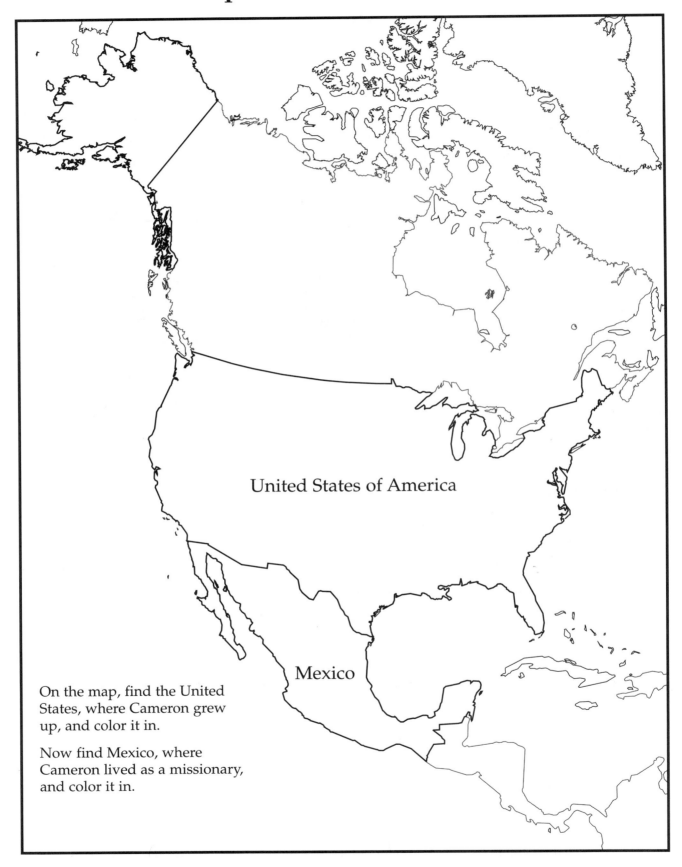

On the map, find the United States, where Cameron grew up, and color it in.

Now find Mexico, where Cameron lived as a missionary, and color it in.

The Flag of Mexico

Above is the flag of Mexico. Color the eagle brown, the snake and surrounding cactus and leaves green, and the rest of the flag green and red where indicated. Leave the middle rectangle white.

Cameron Townsend Quiz

Color the tomatoes whose facts are correct.
Draw a big X over the ones whose facts are incorrect.

- Cameron grew up in a city.
- Cameron knew nothing about farming.
- Cameron went to Guatemala to pass out Spanish Bibles.
- The Guatemalan Indians could all read the Spanish Bibles.
- Cameron learned the Indian languages and created a way to write them down.
- Cameron started a group called Wycliffe to teach others to translate.
- Cameron lived in a Mexican village but never learned the people's language.
- Cameron taught the villagers how to plant new foods and make them grow.
- The mayor in Mexico would not let any of the Wycliffe workers into Mexico.
- Today, over 2,000 Wycliffe workers have helped translate the Bible into other languages.

Fun with Rhyme

It's your turn to be a poet. See if you can fill in the correct word inside each tomato by using the word bank and without looking at your book on Cameron Townsend. Hint: The word will rhyme with the last word in the second line.

Word Bank

clear
pray
seeds
pride
spell
Mark

Cam's father read the Bible to
   his family every day.
They sang a hymn of praise and then
   together they would _____

Cam wondered, *Could I manage to
   develop a good ear*
to hear their language, and then write
   it down so it is _____

The Spanish alphabet, he soon
   decided, would work well.
He'd use the letters to make different
   words that they could _____

So right away Cam set to work,
   from sunrise until dark,
till he could translate Bible chapters
   from the book of _____

And when Cam passed some chapters out,
   the people laughed and cried.
"God speaks our language!" they exclaimed
   with joy and newfound _____

And still today God wants our help—
   the world is filled with needs—
and whether we plant crops or translate,
   we are sowing _____

Cameron Townsend Crossword Puzzle

Word Bank

tortillas
chauffeur
Bible
Wycliffe
mayor
irrigation
California
Mexico
Guatemala
Si

Across

2. A limousine driver.
3. A country that borders the United States.
6. A book that has been translated into many languages.
7. The name of a group of translators.
8. The person who rules a town or village in Mexico.
9. A type of food eaten in Mexico.
10. A way fresh water can flow throughout vegetation.

Down

1. A country in Central America.
4. The state in America where Cameron was from.
5. "Yes" in Spanish.

Lottie Moon: A Generous Offering

Lottie Moon Song

Young Lottie went to China, where she gave so generously. She taught and fed and housed the Chinese people selflessly.

She could not bear to watch the children starve when famine spread, and so she gave her food away so they'd be fed instead.

In China, in China, young Lottie went to China. She dressed just like the people there to show how much she cared.

In China, in China, young Lottie went to China. She loved the people as her own in her adopted home.

The Good Character Quality of Lottie Moon

Definition of Generosity: Freely giving money, time, and talents to help others.

Bible Verse: "Good will come to him who is generous and lends freely" (Psalm 112:5).

Materials

- Copy of the crown, strip, and opal jewel labeled "generosity" on page 64 for each child (use heavy white paper or card stock; if you do not wish to have the children color their crowns, use heavy yellow paper or yellow card stock)
- Scissors
- Crayons or colored pencils
- Stapler
- Double-stick tape or glue

Steps to Follow

1. Introduce the character quality of generosity, which describes Lottie, and discuss its meaning with the children. Read aloud the Bible verse above.

2. Have the children color and cut out the opal labeled "generosity." (Because it is an opal, tell them they may want to color it milky white or pastel.)

3. Have the children color and cut out the crown and strip. Read aloud the following Bible verse: "And when the Chief Shepherd appears, you will receive the crown of glory that will never fade away" (1 Peter 5:4).

4. Have the children tape or glue the opal to the crown. Then have them staple the strip to the crown and put it around their heads. This will serve as their "thinking cap" about generosity.

5. Ask the children, "How did Lottie show generosity in her life through her actions?"
    - Lottie opened up a girls' school in China and taught them how to read and write.
    - Lottie fed, housed, gave out medicine to, and read stories from God's Word to the girls at her school.

- Lottie happily welcomed streams of Chinese visitors into her home and gave them her time.
- Lottie risked her life for an old Chinese man who was being beaten.
- Lottie took in women and children who were poor and all alone, fed them, and gave them medicine.
- Lottie gave her food away when famine spread through China.

6. Ask the children if they know someone—a parent, neighbor, or friend—who demonstrates generosity. Have them tell the class about this person.

7. Ask the children if they can think of examples in their own lives when they have shown generosity or how they would like to be more generous, such as:
   - Giving up a toy to a new boy or girl on the block or in class
   - Letting a brother or sister have first choice of games to play or TV shows to watch
   - Offering the last cookie to someone else
   - Visiting a nursing home to sing for an elderly person or deliver bright pictures you've drawn

8. Have the children sing the character song "We'll Be Generous" on page 65. (This song is sung to the tune of "Do Your Ears Hang Low?" If you have the CD for Lottie Moon, you can have the children follow or sing along with this song. At the end of the CD, there is a solo piano accompaniment that the children can sing along with as well.)

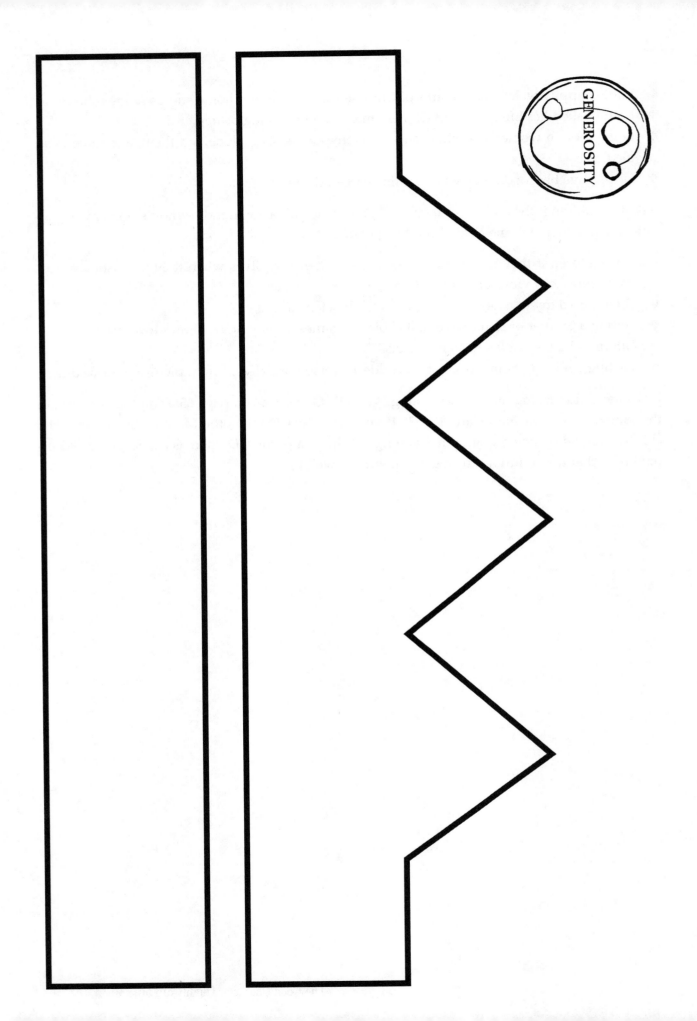

Lottie Moon Character Song
We'll Be Generous

Character Activity for Lottie Moon
Showing Generosity

Materials

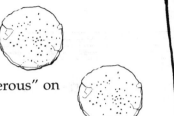

- ❖ Cookies covered in a small basket
- ❖ Bible
- ❖ A copy of the character song "We'll Be Generous" on page 65 for each child

Steps to Follow

1. Have the children demonstrate different emotions you call out: happiness, fear, sadness, and surprise. Ask them to show what their faces would look like and how their bodies would react.

2. Ask the children, "If you were Chinese children who had never seen a white person before and Lottie Moon came to town, how do you think you'd react? Would you feel happy or afraid?"

3. After the children answer, tell them, "I'm going to be Lottie Moon. I'm going to step outside the classroom, and as soon as I come in I want to see on your faces how you feel." Leave the room and get a small basket of cookies that you have kept outside to bring back into the class. (Note: You can also have a student play the role of Lottie Moon.)

4. When you reenter the room, say, "Don't be afraid children. See what I've made from some precious sugar I saved just for you."

5. After passing out the cookies, say, "Let's see on your faces how happy they make you."

6. While the children are eating cookies, read them the Bible verse from Matthew 25:35, which says: "For I was hungry and you gave me something to eat, I was thirsty and you gave me something to drink, I was a stranger and you invited me in, I needed clothes and you clothed me, I was sick and you looked after me."

7. When the children have finished eating, hand out a copy of the song "We'll Be Generous" to each child and say, "Lottie Moon was very generous in her life, not only by making cookies for the Chinese children but by giving her own food away when there was a famine in the land and the children were starving, even though it meant that she had to go hungry instead. Let's sing the song 'We'll Be Generous.'"

Caution: Some children, because of health reasons, should not be given certain foods. Please take all necessary precautions, including asking each child's parent or guardian for permission to give the child cookies.

Shoebox Activity for Lottie Moon
How We Can Be Generous

Materials

- The sun, moon, and star patterns on the following page copied onto white construction paper for each child (or use blank yellow, white, and blue construction paper for older children)
- Colored pencils or crayons
- Silver and gold glitter glue
- Scissors
- Regular glue or double-stick tape
- Three popsicle or craft sticks for each child
- Copy of the character song "We'll Be Generous" on page 65 for each child
- Newspaper (to cover the table surface)

Steps to Follow

1. Review ways the children can be generous, such as:
   - Giving up a toy to a new boy or girl on the block or in class
   - Letting a brother or sister have first choice of games to play or TV shows to watch
   - Offering the last cookie to someone else
   - Visiting a nursing home to sing for an elderly person or delivering bright pictures you've drawn

2. Have the children color their sun, moon, and star patterns. For older children, have them create their own designs on yellow, white, and blue construction paper.

3. Have them cut out their sun, moon, and star.

4. Have them put gold glitter glue on their sun and moon, and silver glitter glue on their star.

5. Have them glue or tape each pattern to a popsicle or craft stick.

6. Now have the children take turns standing up and saying, "My light is like the moon (or sun or star). I will let God's light shine generously through me by…."

7. Sing the character song "We'll Be Generous" while the children hold up their suns, moons, and stars.

8. Have the children put their suns, moons, and stars in their shoeboxes as a reminder of how Lottie Moon was a light for God in China.

Chinese Paper Fan

On hot days in China, both men and women use a paper fan, or *shan*, to keep cool. The fans have lovely paintings or designs on them.

Materials

- One 12 x 18 inch piece of white paper for each child
- Crayons, colored pencils, or markers
- Clear tape

Steps to Follow

1. Place the paper horizontally so that the long side is the bottom edge in front of you. Use crayons, markers, or colored pencils to draw a colorful scene or design on the top half of the paper. Leave a small margin in the middle of the page (see diagram).

2. Turn the paper around and draw a picture on the other top half (on the same side of the sheet).

3. Accordion-fold the paper into equal sections.

4. Pinch the pleated paper in the center. Bring up the two up-facing sides and tape them together in the middle into a fan shape.

5. Fold the bottom center of the paper into a handle and fold out the fan all the way.

Map: Lottie Moon

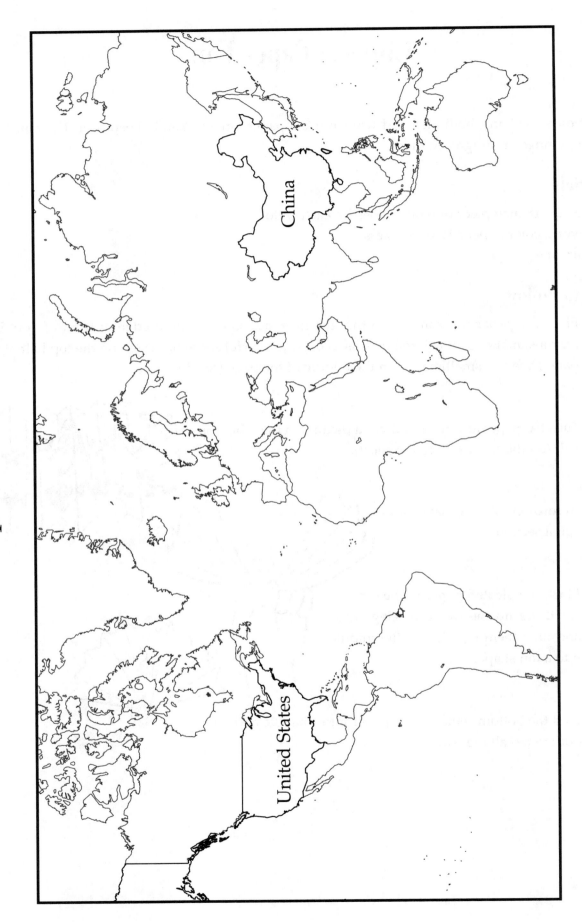

On the map, find the United States, where Lottie grew up, and color it in.

Now find China, where Lottie lived as a missionary, and color it in.

The Flag of China

Above is the flag of China. Color the stars yellow and the rest of the flag bright red.

Lottie Moon Quiz

Color the fans whose facts are correct.
Draw a big X over the fans whose facts are incorrect.

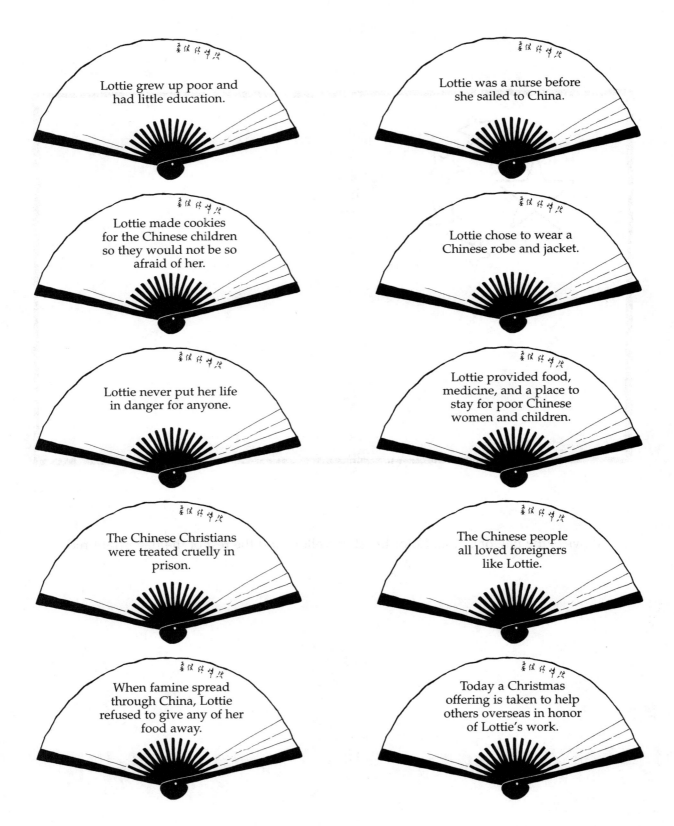

Fun with Rhyme

It's your turn to be a poet. See if you can fill in the correct word inside each fan by using the word bank and without looking at your book on Lottie Moon. Hint: The word will rhyme with the last word in the second line.

Word Bank

love
rods
know
knew
meet
head

Young Lottie, who loved teaching, was
    convinced that she should go,
since most Chinese had not heard of
    the God that we all _____

As word spread that the nephew would
    not worship their old gods,
a group of angry men attacked
    him with some bamboo _____

Her hair, once in a bun, was now
    a long pigtail instead.
She wore a business person's robe,
    a skullcap on her _____

And yet she was not welcomed by
    the neighbors on her street.
They disliked foreigners and were
    unfriendly when they'd _____

Just as the moon reflects the sun,
    so Lottie Moon shone too;
she let her light shine in His name
    with everyone she _____

Like Lottie Moon, we too can choose
    to serve the Lord above.
We too can be a light for God,
    reflecting His great _____

Lottie Moon Crossword Puzzle

Word Bank

famine
Moon
bamboo
teacher
America
China
Testament
robe
panda
Mandarin

Across

3. The country Lottie was from.
4. A type of bear found in China.
5. The country in Asia where Lottie worked as a missionary.
6. Lottie gave an old Chinese man a New _ _ _ _ _ _ _ _ _.
7. A type of plant in China.
9. A type of clothing the Chinese wear.

Down

1. A food shortage.
2. The language Lottie learned in China.
6. What Lottie trained to become before she went to China.
8. Lottie _ _ _ _.

Can You Name the Hero?

See if you can write the correct name of each hero in the space provided from the clues in each verse.

Can you name the hero who learned how to create
    new letters for new languages to help him to translate?
Can you name this man who started something new:
    a group called Wycliffe that trains others how to translate too?

    His name was _____. He started Wycliffe.

Can you name the hero who left for Ecuador
    to work among the Indians and teach about our Lord?
Can you name this man who, since his sacrifice,
    has inspired many, many thousands with his life?

    His name was _____. He was a light for God.

Can you name the hero who opened up her home
    to the Chinese who were poor or hungry or alone?
Can you name this woman who gave, when famine spread,
    her food away to the Chinese so they'd be fed instead?

    Her name was _____. She gave so generously.

Can you name the hero who had a great big dream
    and finished Bible school, though his classmates had been mean?
Can you name this man who preached when he was blind,
    because he loved the Lord our God with all his heart and mind?

    His name was _____. He never would give up.

Note: This exercise can also be sung by following along on the companion CD for books 13–16. When the chorus is repeated the second time, the answers are included.

Answers to "Can You Name the Hero?"

1. Cameron Townsend
2. Jim Elliot
3. Lottie Moon
4. Jonathan Goforth

Answers to Questions

Answers to Jim Elliot

Jim Elliot Quiz: Correct Facts

- Jim learned to speak Spanish and a tribal language in Ecuador.
- Jim lost his hut, clinic, and part of the airstrip and school during a terrible rainstorm.
- Jim wanted to reach out to the Aucas and tell them about God.
- The Auca Indians did not welcome outsiders.
- Years after Jim was killed, many Aucas became Christians.

Fun with Rhyme

1. need
2. few
3. ground
4. say
5. out
6. shine

Crossword

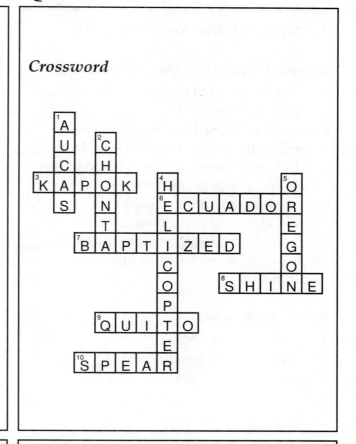

Answers to Jonathan Goforth

Jonathan Goforth Quiz: Correct Facts

- Jonathan grew up quite poor on a farm in the country.
- Jonathan visited the slums and prison to tell about God's love.
- Jonathan's classmates decided to support him as a missionary.
- Thousands came to hear Jonathan teach and preach in China.
- Jonathan became blind when he was 73.
- Though Jonathan was laughed at during his life, he had continued to do God's work.

Fun with Rhyme

1. go
2. Son
3. met
4. good
5. sun
6. right

Crossword

Answers to Cameron Townsend

Cameron Townsend Quiz: Correct Facts

- Cameron went to Guatemala to pass out Spanish Bibles.
- Cameron learned the Indian languages and created a way to write them down.
- Cameron started a group called Wycliffe to teach others to translate.
- Cameron taught the villagers how to plant new foods and make them grow.
- Today, over 2,000 Wycliffe workers have helped translate the Bible into other languages.

Fun with Rhyme

1. pray
2. clear
3. spell
4. Mark
5. pride
6. seeds

Crossword

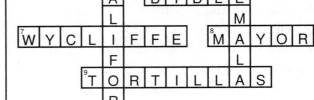

Answers to Lottie Moon

Lottie Moon Quiz: Correct Facts

- Lottie made cookies for the Chinese children so they would not be so afraid of her.
- Lottie chose to wear a Chinese robe and jacket.
- Lottie provided food, medicine, and a place to stay for poor Chinese women and children.
- The Chinese Christians were treated cruelly in prison.
- Today a Christmas offering is taken to help others overseas in honor of Lottie's work.

Fun with Rhyme

1. know
2. rods
3. head
4. meet
5. knew
6. love

Crossword

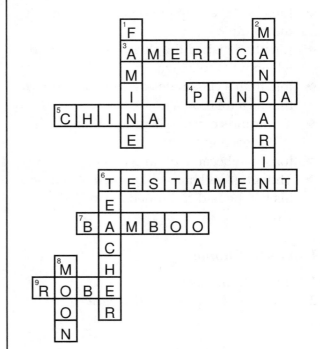

I Will Follow

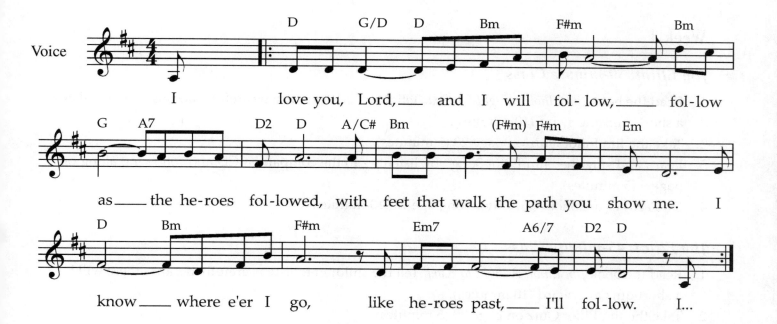

2. I love You, Lord, and I will follow,
   follow as the heroes followed,
   with hands that help in ways You guide me.
   I know where e'er I go,
   like heroes past, I'll follow.

3. I love You, Lord, and I will follow,
   follow as the heroes followed,
   with ears that hear the truth You tell me.
   I know where e'er I go,
   like heroes past, I'll follow.

4. I love You, Lord, and I will follow,
   follow as the heroes followed,
   with eyes that see the needs around me.
   I know where e'er I go,
   like heroes past, I'll follow.

Syllabus

Week 1

Jim Elliot: 30-minute Class

1. Read the book *Jim Elliot: A Light for God*. Tell the children to listen carefully because there will be a short quiz afterward (10 minutes).
2. Take the Jim Elliot Quiz on page 20 (5 minutes).
3. Learn and sing the "Jim Elliot Song" by listening to the companion CD and following along on page 9 (5 minutes).
4. Do Part I of the Shoebox Activity on page 15 (10 minutes).

Jim Elliot: 45-minute Class

1. Read the book *Jim Elliot: A Light for God*. Tell the children to listen carefully because there will be a short quiz afterward (10 minutes).
2. Take the Jim Elliot Quiz on page 20 (5 minutes).
3. Learn and sing the "Jim Elliot Song" by listening to the companion CD and following along on page 9 (5 minutes).
4. Do Part I and Part II of the Shoebox Activity on pages 15–16 (25 minutes).

Week 2

Jim Elliot: 30-minute Class

1. Review the "Jim Elliot Song" on page 9 (5 minutes).
2. Learn and sing the Character Song "We Will Be Devoted" on page 13 (5 minutes).
3. Do Part II of the Shoebox Activity on pages 15–16 (20 minutes).

Jim Elliot: 45-minute Class

1. Review the "Jim Elliot Song" on page 9 (5 minutes).
2. Learn about the Good Character Quality of Jim on pages 10–11 (15 minutes) and sing the Character Song "We Will Be Devoted" on page 13 (5 minutes).
3. Do the Character Activity on page 14 (20 minutes).

Week 3

Jonathan Goforth: 30-minute Class

1. Read the book *Jonathan Goforth: Never Give Up* (10 minutes).

2. Learn and sing the "Jonathan Goforth Song" by listening to the companion CD and following along on page 25 (5 minutes).
3. Do the Character Activity on page 30 (15 minutes).

Jonathan Goforth: 45-minute Class

1. Read the book *Jonathan Goforth: Never Give Up* (10 minutes).
2. Learn and sing the "Jonathan Goforth Song" by listening to the companion CD and following along on page 25 (5 minutes).
3. Learn about the Good Character Quality of Jonathan on pages 26–27 (10 minutes) and sing the Character Song "We Will Be Determined" on page 29 (5 minutes).
4. Do the Character Activity on page 30 (15 minutes).

Week 4

Jonathan Goforth: 30-minute Class

1. Review the "Jonathan Goforth Song" on page 25 (5 minutes).
2. Learn and sing the Character Song "We Will Be Determined" on page 29 (5 minutes).
3. Do the Shoebox Activity on page 31 (20 minutes).

Jonathan Goforth: 45-minute Class

1. Review the "Jonathan Goforth Song" on page 25 (5 minutes).
2. Review the Character Song "We Will Be Determined" on page 29 (5 minutes).
3. Take the Jonathan Goforth Quiz on page 39 (5 minutes).
4. Do the Shoebox Activity on page 31 (20 minutes).
5. Color the Jonathan Goforth map on page 37 and the flag of Canada on page 38 (10 minutes).

Week 5

Cameron Townsend: 30-minute Class

1. Read the book *Cameron Townsend: Planting God's Word* (10 minutes).
2. Learn and sing the "Cameron Townsend Song" by listening to the companion CD and following along on page 45 (5 minutes).
3. Do the Character Activity on page 50 (15 minutes).

Cameron Townsend: 45-minute Class

1. Read the book *Cameron Townsend: Planting God's Word* (10 minutes).
2. Learn and sing the "Cameron Townsend Song" by listening to the companion CD and following along on page 45 (5 minutes).

3. Learn about the Good Character Quality of Cameron on pages 46–47 (10 minutes) and sing the Character Song "We Will Be Resourceful" on page 49 (5 minutes).
4. Do the Character Activity on page 50 (15 minutes).

Week 6

Cameron Townsend: 30-minute Class

1. Review the "Cameron Townsend Song" on page 45 (5 minutes).
2. Do the Shoebox Activity on page 51 (25 minutes).

Cameron Townsend: 45-minute Class

1. Review the "Cameron Townsend Song" on page 45 (5 minutes).
2. Review the Character Song "We Will Be Resourceful" on page 49 (5 minutes).
3. Do the Shoebox Activity on page 51 (25 minutes).
4. Color the Cameron Townsend picture on page 43 (10 minutes).
   Optional: While the children are coloring, play the "Cameron Townsend Song," "We Will Be Resourceful," and "I Will Follow" from the companion CD for them to listen to.

Week 7

Lottie Moon: 30-minute Class

1. Read the book *Lottie Moon: A Generous Offering*. Tell the children to listen carefully because there will be a short quiz afterward (10 minutes).
2. Take the Lottie Moon Quiz on page 72 (5 minutes).
3. Learn and sing the "Lottie Moon Song" by listening to the companion CD and following along on page 61 (5 minutes).
4. Do the Character Activity on page 66 (10 minutes).

Lottie Moon: 45-minute Class

1. Read the book *Lottie Moon: A Generous Offering*. Tell the children to listen carefully because there will be a short quiz afterward (10 minutes).
2. Take the Lottie Moon Quiz on page 72 (5 minutes).
3. Learn and sing the "Lottie Moon Song" by listening to the companion CD and following along on page 61 (5 minutes).
4. Learn about the Good Character Quality of Lottie on pages 62–63 (10 minutes) and sing the Character Song "We'll Be Generous" on page 65 (5 minutes).
5. Do the Character Activity on page 66 (10 minutes).

Week 8

Lottie Moon: 30-minute Class

1. Review the "Lottie Moon Song" on page 61 (5 minutes).
2. Do the Shoebox Activity on page 67 (25 minutes).

Lottie Moon: 45-minute Class

1. Review the "Lottie Moon Song" on page 61 (5 minutes).
2. Do Fun with Rhyme on page 73 (5 minutes).
3. Do the Shoebox Activity on page 67 (25 minutes).
4. Color the Lottie Moon picture on page 59 (10 minutes).
   Optional: While the children are coloring, play the "Lottie Moon Song," "We'll Be Generous," and "I Will Follow" from the companion CD for them to listen to.

Week 9

Jim Elliot: 30-minute Class

1. Reread the book *Jim Elliot: A Light for God* (10 minutes).
2. Do the Character Activity on page 14 (20 minutes).

Jim Elliot: 45-minute Class

1. Reread the book *Jim Elliot: A Light for God* (10 minutes).
2. Review the "Jim Elliot Song" on page 9 and/or the Character Song "We Will Be Devoted" on page 13 (5 minutes).
3. Work the Crossword Puzzle on page 22 (10 minutes).
4. Color the Jim Elliot map on page 18 and/or the flag of Ecuador on page 19 (5 minutes).
5. Do Fun with Rhyme on page 21 (5 minutes).
6. Color the Jim Elliot picture on page 7 (10 minutes).
   Optional: While the children are coloring, play the "Jim Elliot Song," "We Will Be Devoted," and "I Will Follow" from the companion CD for them to listen to.

Week 10

Jonathan Goforth: 30-minute Class

1. Reread the book *Jonathan Goforth: Never Give Up*. Tell the children to listen carefully because there will be a short quiz afterward (10 minutes).
2. Take the Jonathan Goforth Quiz on page 39 (5 minutes).

3. Review the "Jonathan Goforth Song" on page 25 and/or the Character Song "We Will Be Determined" on page 29 (5 minutes).
4. Color the Jonathan Goforth picture on page 23 (10 minutes).
   Optional: While the children are coloring, play the "Jonathan Goforth Song," "We Will Be Determined," and "I Will Follow" from the companion CD for them to listen to.

Jonathan Goforth: 45-minute Class

1. Reread the book *Jonathan Goforth: Never Give Up* (10 minutes).
2. Work the Crossword Puzzle on page 41 (10 minutes).
3. Make the Canadian beaver on pages 33–34 (15 minutes).
4. Color the Jonathan Goforth picture on page 23 (10 minutes).
   Optional: While the children are coloring, play the "Jonathan Goforth Song," "We Will Be Determined," and "I Will Follow" from the companion CD for them to listen to.

Week 11

Cameron Townsend: 30-minute Class

1. Reread the book *Cameron Townsend: Planting God's Word*. Tell the children to listen carefully because there will be a short quiz afterward (10 minutes).
2. Take the Cameron Townsend Quiz on page 56 (5 minutes).
3. Review the "Cameron Townsend Song" on page 45 and/or the Character Song "We Will Be Resourceful" on page 49 (5 minutes).
4. Color the Cameron Townsend picture on page 43 (10 minutes).
   Optional: While the children are coloring, play the "Cameron Townsend Song," "We Will Be Resourceful," and "I Will Follow" from the companion CD for them to listen to.

Cameron Townsend: 45-minute Class

1. Reread the book *Cameron Townsend: Planting God's Word*. Tell the children to listen carefully because there will be a short quiz afterward (10 minutes).
2. Take the Cameron Townsend Quiz on page 56 (5 minutes).
3. Make a piñata on page 53 (30 minutes).

Week 12

Lottie Moon: 30-minute Class

1. Reread the book *Lottie Moon: A Generous Offering* (10 minutes).
2. Make the Chinese paper fan on page 69 (20 minutes).

Lottie Moon: 45-minute Class

1. Reread the book *Lottie Moon: A Generous Offering* (10 minutes).
2. Review the "Lottie Moon Song" on page 61 and/or the Character Song "We'll Be Generous" on page 65 (5 minutes).
3. Work the Crossword Puzzle on page 74 (10 minutes).
4. Make the Chinese paper fan on page 69 (20 minutes).

Week 13

30-minute Class

1. Sing the "Can You Name the Hero?" song by listening to the companion CD and following along on page 75 (5 minutes).
2. Read the definitions of the character traits on each of the Good Character Quality pages and see if the children can guess the trait and the name of the hero that the trait applies to (5 minutes).
3. Play the game "Who Am I?" Have each child pick the name of one of the four heroes from a basket and have them act out who that hero is. For Lottie Moon, for example, a child might pretend to serve the other children cookies; for Cameron Townsend, a child might pretend to plant seeds. Let the rest of the class try to guess who the hero is (10 minutes).
4. Have each child pick the name of one of the four heroes from a basket and draw a picture that makes others think of that hero, e.g., a parrot, tomato, fan or panda bear (10 minutes).

45-minute Class

1. Sing the "Can You Name the Hero?" song by listening to the companion CD and following along on page 75 (5 minutes).
2. Read the definitions of the character traits on each of the Good Character Quality pages and see if the children can guess the trait and the name of the hero that the trait applies to (5 minutes).
3. Play the game "Who Am I?" Have each child pick the name of one of the four heroes from a basket and have them act out who that hero is. For Lottie Moon, for example, a child might pretend to serve the other children cookies; for Cameron Townsend, a child might pretend to plant seeds. Let the rest of the class try to guess who the hero is (10 minutes).
4. Have each child pick the name of one of the four heroes from a basket and draw a picture that makes others think of that hero, e.g., a parrot, tomato, or panda bear (10 minutes).
5. Tell who your favorite hero is and why (5 minutes).
6. Ask the children to pick their favorite songs and sing them (10 minutes).

Notes

Heroes for Young Readers

Written by Renee Taft Meloche • Illustrated by Bryan Pollard

Don't miss the exciting stories of other Christian heroes! Whether reading for themselves or being read to, children love the captivating rhyming text and unforgettable color illustrations of the Heroes for Young Readers series. See the next page for more Activity Guides and CDs.

BOOKS 1–4

Gladys Aylward: Daring to Trust • Trust in God enabled Gladys Aylward (1902–1970) to safely lead nearly one hundred Chinese orphans on a daring journey that saved their lives. ISBN 1-57658-228-0

Nate Saint: Heavenbound • Nate Saint (1923–1956) flew his plane over the jungles of Ecuador, helping missionaries reach isolated Indians with God's great love. ISBN 1-57658-229-9

Eric Liddell: Running for a Higher Prize • From winning Olympic gold as a runner to leaving his fame in Scotland behind to go to China as a missionary, Eric Liddell (1902–1945) put God in first place. ISBN 1-57658-230-2

George Müller: Faith to Feed Ten Thousand • George Müller (1805–1898) opened an orphanage, trusting God to faithfully provide for the needs of thousands of England's orphaned children. ISBN 1-57658-232-9

BOOKS 5–8

Corrie ten Boom: Shining in the Darkness • Corrie ten Boom (1892–1983) and her family risked everything to extend God's hand of love and protection to their Jewish neighbors during WWII. ISBN 1-57658-231-0

Amy Carmichael: Rescuing the Children • Amy Carmichael (1867–1951) rescued hundreds of women and children, first in Irish slums and then in India, by fearing God and nothing else. ISBN 1-57658-233-7

Mary Slessor: Courage in Africa • Mary Slessor (1848–1915) courageously shared Jesus' life and freedom with the unreached tribes of Africa's Calabar region. ISBN 1-57658-237-X

William Carey: Bearer of Good News • William Carey (1761–1834) left England behind and sailed to faraway India, where he devoted himself to translating the Bible into the native languages. ISBN 1-57658-236-1

BOOKS 9–12

Hudson Taylor: Friend of China • Known as one of the greatest pioneer missionaries of all time, Hudson Taylor (1832–1905) overcame huge obstacles to reach the Chinese. ISBN 1-57658-234-5

David Livingstone: Courageous Explorer • Trailblazing explorer David Livingstone (1813–1873) would not let anything stand in his way as he mapped unexplored Africa and healed the sick. ISBN 1-57658-238-8

Adoniram Judson: A Grand Purpose • Even imprisonment could not stop America's first foreign missionary, Adoniram Judson (1788–1850), as he translated the Bible into Burmese. ISBN 1-57658-240-X

Betty Greene: Flying High • Betty Greene (1920–1997) combined her love of flying with her love for Christ by helping found the Mission Aviation Fellowship. ISBN 1-57658-239-6

BOOKS 13–16

Lottie Moon: A Generous Offering • As a missionary to some of the poorest cities in China, once-wealthy Lottie Moon (1840–1912) experienced having nothing to eat. In dire circumstances, Lottie's first priority was teaching others about God's love. ISBN 1-57658-243-4

Jim Elliot: A Light for God • Jim Elliot (1927–1956) bravely faced both the wonders and the dangers of the South American jungle to share God's love with the feared and isolated Auca people. ISBN 1-57658-235-3

Jonathan Goforth: Never Give Up • In faraway China, despite danger and ridicule, Jonathan Goforth (1859–1936) and his wife generously opened their home to thousands of Chinese visitors, sharing the Good News of the gospel. ISBN 1-57658-242-6

Cameron Townsend: Planting God's Word • After planting God's Word in the hearts of people all over Guatemala and Mexico, Cameron Townsend (1896–1982) started Wycliffe Bible Translators so that all people could read the Good News for themselves. ISBN 1-57658-241-8

(over)

Heroes for Young Readers Activity Guides and CDs
by Renee Taft Meloche

Whether for home, school, or Sunday school, don't miss these fun-filled Activity Guides and CDs presenting the lives of other Heroes for Young Readers.

Heroes for Young Readers Activity Guides
For Books 1–4: Gladys Aylward, Eric Liddell, Nate Saint, George Müller • 1-57658-367-8
For Books 5–8: Amy Carmichael, Corrie ten Boom, Mary Slessor, William Carey • 1-57658-368-6
For Books 9–12: Betty Greene, David Livingstone, Adoniram Judson, Hudson Taylor • 1-57658-369-4
For Books 13–16: Jim Elliot, Jonathan Goforth, Cameron Townsend, Lottie Moon • 1-57658-370-8

Heroes for Young Readers Activity Audio CD
Each Activity Guide has an available audio CD with book readings, songs, and fun activity tracks, helping you to get the most out of the Activity Guides!

CD for Books 1–4 • 1-57658-396-1
CD for Books 5–8 • 1-57658-397-X
CD for Books 9–12 • 1-57658-398-8
CD for Books 13–16 • 1-57658-399-6

Heroes for Young Readers Activity Guide Package Special
Includes the Activity Guide, audio CD, and four corresponding Heroes for Young Readers hardcover books.

For Books 1–4 Package • 1-57658-375-9
For Books 5–8 Package • 1-57658-376-7
For Books 9–12 Package • 1-57658-377-5
For Books 13–16 Package • 1-57658-378-3

Christian Heroes: Then & Now
by Janet and Geoff Benge

The Heroes for Young Readers books are based on the Christian Heroes: Then & Now biographies by Janet and Geoff Benge. Discover these exciting, true adventures for ages ten and up! Many unit study curriculum guides for older students are also available to accompany these biographies.

Gladys Aylward: The Adventure of a Lifetime • 1-57658-019-9
Nate Saint: On a Wing and a Prayer • 1-57658-017-2
Hudson Taylor: Deep in the Heart of China • 1-57658-016-4
Amy Carmichael: Rescuer of Precious Gems • 1-57658-018-0
Eric Liddell: Something Greater Than Gold • 1-57658-137-3
Corrie ten Boom: Keeper of the Angels' Den • 1-57658-136-5
William Carey: Obliged to Go • 1-57658-147-0
George Müller: The Guardian of Bristol's Orphans • 1-57658-145-4
Jim Elliot: One Great Purpose • 1-57658-146-2
Mary Slessor: Forward into Calabar • 1-57658-148-9
David Livingstone: Africa's Trailblazer • 1-57658-153-5
Betty Greene: Wings to Serve • 1-57658-152-7
Adoniram Judson: Bound for Burma • 1-57658-161-6
Cameron Townsend: Good News in Every Language • 1-57658-164-0
Jonathan Goforth: An Open Door in China • 1-57658-174-8
Lottie Moon: Giving Her All for China • 1-57658-188-8

...and many more!

For a free catalog of books and materials contact
YWAM Publishing, P.O. Box 55787, Seattle, WA 98155
1-800-922-2143, www.ywampublishing.com